Printed in the United Kingdom.

First Printing, 2018

Paperback ISBN: 978-1-9165025-3-6
eBook ISBN: 978-1-9165025-0-5

Sea Salt Publishing

Bournemouth, Dorset

seasaltlearning.com

julianstodd.wordpress.com

THE SOCIAL LEARNING GUIDEBOOK

A Guide for Learning Transformation

By Julian Stodd

INTRODUCTION

This short *Social Learning Guidebook* is intended to highlight areas that you should consider when you look at learning transformation. It is not intended to have all the answers, but rather to offer some frameworks and models that you may want to adopt, and include activities that you can do along the way.

Every section includes boxed descriptions related to *'What you should know'*, and *'What you should do'*. These are not definitive, but intended to help you take the first steps.

This guidebook is the first of several guides to Learning Transformation. The next one will be 'The Community Handbook', and will explore how to create the right conditions for learning communities to thrive. If you are particularly interested in this work, check out more on my blog, 'Learning Architecture'.

My previous work on 'Learning Methodology' [2013] covers more about the underlying learning science and pedagogy. If that's something you're interested in, be sure to check it out!

This book, like much of my work, is intended to iterate rapidly as my own understanding evolves, and to be rapidly disposable, as our research and practice within Sea Salt Learning develops.

For now, however, I hope that this book will contribute to your efforts to transform your Organisation.

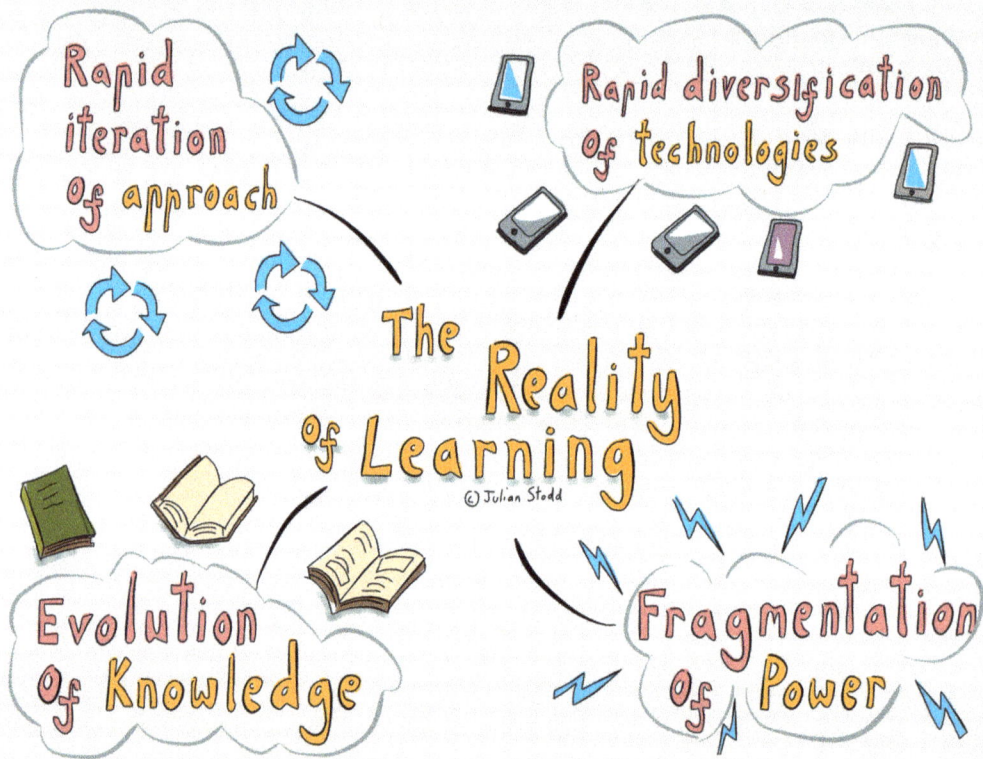

The Reality of Learning

Rapid iteration of approach

Rapid diversification of technologies

Evolution of Knowledge

Fragmentation of Power

© Julian Stodd

You can read more about Social Learning, and about the wider evolution of learning on my blog at www.julianstodd.wordpress.com

OVERVIEW

Social Learning is a story partly written by the learners themselves. It's about tacit, tribal, lived wisdom; It's the learning that exists within distributed communities. It is often untidy, diverse, and deeply personal, as people bring their own perspective and experiences into it. Moreover, it's the mechanism by which we really learn and further, learn to be effective.

Modern organisations are increasingly interested in how to unlock the power of Social Learning. This increasing interest shows that organisations are beginning to recognise that, fundamentally, learning is changing, and so too must our approach to its design and facilitation.

In this Guidebook , we will explore what Social Learning is, and consider a design methodology of 'Scaffolded Social Learning' [Stodd, 2014].

Social Learning Ecosystem
© Julian Stodd

Organisations capture their codified strength in formal stories

They share these stories through formal learning

They use technology for distribution, assessment, and compliance

Formal Learning is great for driving consistency, conformity, and standardised strength.

Social Learning is great for building a Diversified Strength and individual capability

They carry out 'sense making' activities

For Social Learning, Communities take the formal story and add local and individual context.

We can create spaces and provide support for this to happen, using Scaffolded Social Learning approaches.

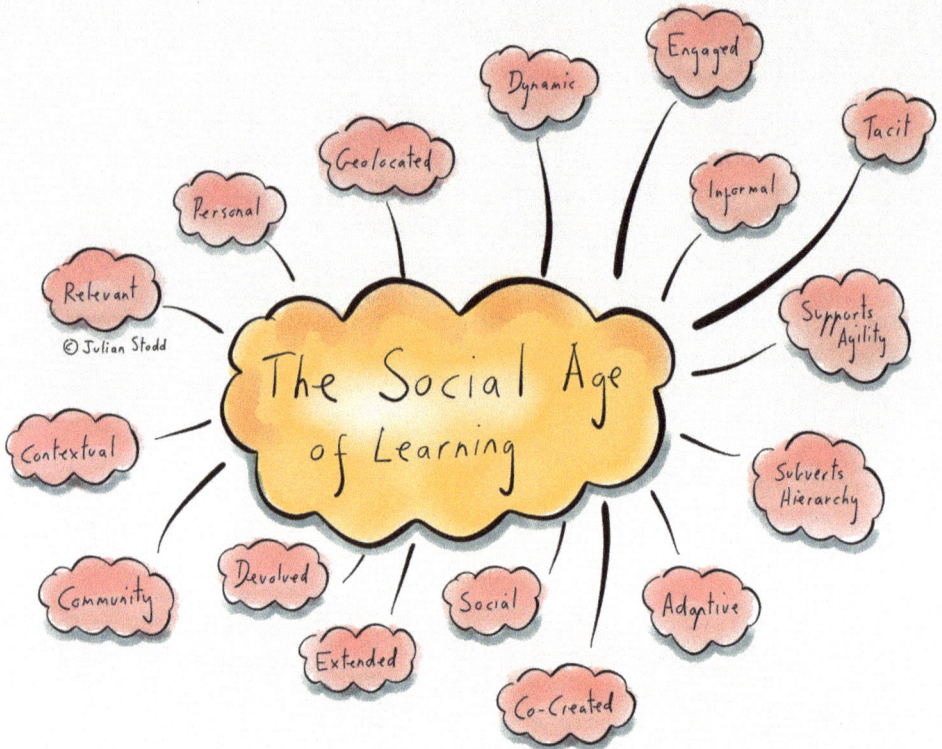

The Social Age of Learning

(clouds: Engaged, Dynamic, Geolocated, Tacit, Personal, Informal, Relevant, Supports Agility, Contextual, Subverts Hierarchy, Community, Devolved, Social, Adaptive, Extended, Co-Created)

© Julian Stodd

We will do this within the context of the Social Age, the new ecosystem in which we live, to help us better understand the impact that the Social Age has on learning, through its evolved forms of power, knowledge, and control.

We will consider the communities within which Social Learning occurs: what they are, how they form, where they exist, how they are moderated, and what we can do to create the conditions for them to thrive.

Stories are the basic mechanism for the cultural transmission of information:
Thus, we will examine how stories are both co-created and used in Social Learning, and further consider the relationship between the personal stories of individual learners, the collaborative stories of communities, and the stories that organisations themselves tell.

Finally, we will consider the cultural shift: how Social Learning is part of the broader changes that erode the power of formal structures, and empower social ones. In other words, we will explore the way in which a '*learning organisation*' may evolve a culture to gain a competitive edge, as well as how the learning itself may be done more by the organisation than each of the individual learners.

Formal learning is a story written by an organisation, and 'done' to people. *Social Learning is a story where everyone has a voice;* It's measurable, effective, and highly dynamic. Nevertheless, to truly reap the benefits of this learning, change is necessary. Indeed, we need to transform how we design, deliver, support, and facilitate learning, as well as change how we hear the stories that are told.

SUMMARY

....

WHAT YOU NEED TO KNOW:

- *Social Learning is an approach to learning that combines the 'formal' story of the organisation, with the 'social' stories from the community.*

- *Social Learning itself is an indicator of a broader cultural transformation, a shift in the way the organisation itself learns.*

- *The 'Social Age' is the context within which Social Learning occurs. It is an evolved ecosystem, delivering different powers, drivers, and capabilities.*

NOTES

FOUNDATIONS OF THE SOCIAL AGE

Something about the current era is driving this move towards Social Learning. In this section, we will consider the context of the Social Age, and the impact it has on learning and learning culture.

Technology is the most visible manifestation of change. In recent years, we have seen a rise in social collaborative technologies, which have led to the proliferation of connectivity and the democratisation of organisation. *Put simply, we are now connected in many different ways, almost all of which are outside the oversight or control of any formal organisation or entity.* In terms of network, there is a high level of resilience and redundancy in our connections.

This connectivity is significant: Historically, mechanisms of connection were either local and tribal, or large-scale and formal. In the past, we were connected within formal hierarchies and formal organisations, and within those spaces we were expected to conform (to wear the '*uniform*', to use the appropriate '*language*', to accept the imposition of '*control*'). Today, that global connection (i.e. social collaborative connection at scale) is broadly social, and with this shift comes a shift in the various types of power at play, individual expectations, a sense of entitlement, and perception towards fairness.

In turn, this connectivity leads to a shift in power (individual, collective, and formal); There is a broad rebalancing of power in the Social Age – away from formal systems (hierarchy) and towards social ones (community). In a world of democratised connectivity, socially amplified storytelling, and the distributed validation of knowledge, one person can hold a formal organisation, or even the government, accountable. Or at least, they can if their story is authentic, socially validated, and shared in a compelling manner.

An important part of the context of the Social Age is the fracturing of the Social Contract between the individual and the organisation, where the notion of 'career' is dead, and where the only 'constants' we maintain are our personal networks and the broader communities that we live within. This has serious implications for engagement. Looking ahead, new 'Guilds' are likely to emerge [Stodd 2018]; These 'Guilds' will be cooperatively organised, collectively powerful, the backbones of our professional development, and they will exist beyond any formal organisation.

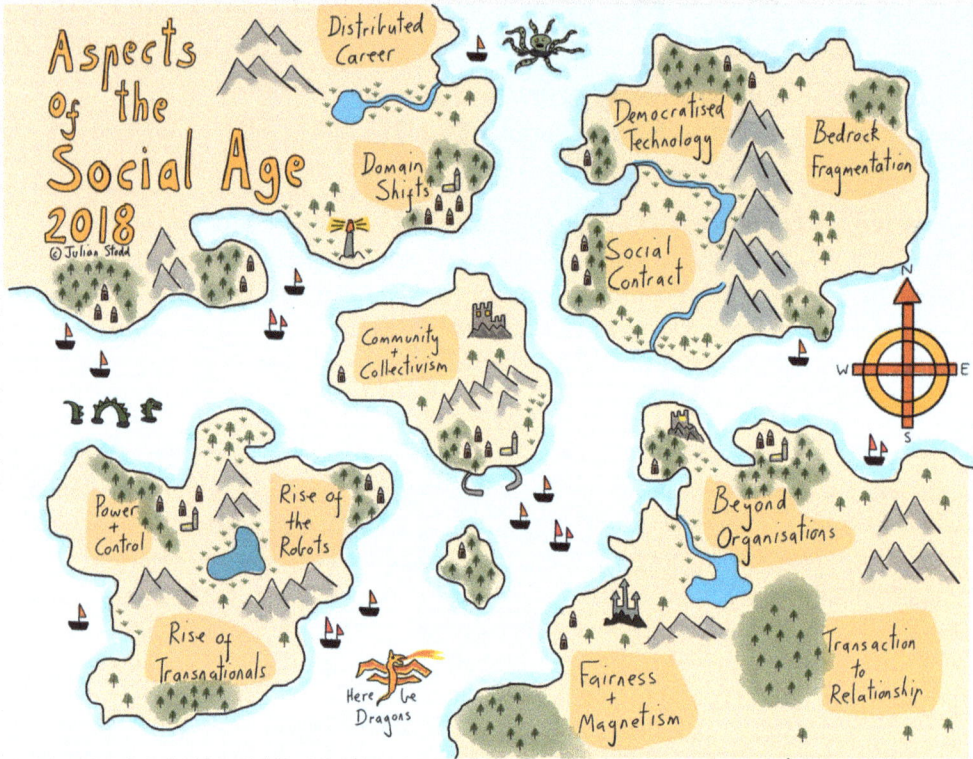

Aspects of the Social Age 2018
© Julian Stodd

(map labels: Distributed Career, Domain Shifts, Democratised Technology, Bedrock Fragmentation, Social Contract, Community + Collectivism, Power + Control, Rise of the Robots, Beyond Organisations, Rise of Transnationals, Here be Dragons, Fairness + Magnetism, Transaction to Relationship)

As organisations no longer provide the ongoing structure of our personal development, *new entities will emerge, or adapt, to fill this space.* Many of them will be socially moderated and likely use Social Learning approaches.

We have already seen the early stages of this: Massive Open Online Courses (the MOOCs, which represent democratised teaching), the tech entities like LinkedIn and Udemy (democratised, beyond formal control), and the emergent Guilds (emergent political powers, crossing within and beyond the boundaries of the organisation, holding domain-specific knowledge and capabilities e.g. Cybersecurity). However, the type of learning they bring us is different. This type of learning is no longer hindered by decades of stagnation and 'known knowledge'; Instead, it is typically more dynamic, co-created, contextual, adaptive, and free.

Ecosystem of Organisation

© Julian Stodd

Evolved structures of **Education** for continuous Learning

Professionally engaged, through the new **Guilds** which themselves forge Organisational links

Connected in different and unified **Tribes** which build their own culture

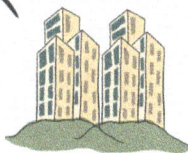

Lightweight **Organisations** which hold brand value and earn customer and team loyalty

This speaks to the challenge of how organisations adapt to the changing environment within which they exist: Clinging to old models of Organisational Design (nested power structures), formal learning (learning as a form of control), formal hierarchies of power (systems of consequence), and known knowledge (unchallenging, static) is a sure-fire way to be disrupted (Black Swans/VUCA) [Stodd, Reitz, 2015]. From the level of organisations to the level of Nations themselves, the old methods, rules, and 'ways of doing things' are becoming out-dated.

Enabled by democratised technology and the proliferation of informal learning, the dominant modes of social organisation are also evolving. Historically, human beings were organised into villages, towns, cities, and tribes, all geographically determined, in which culture was tied to specific place. But today, the limitation of geography is all but eliminated as a result of collaborative technology, and culture is no longer tied to a specific place. I can as easily be a Citizen of Apple in the State of Lego, as i can a citizen of my own State.

We are used to seeing learning as a discrete part of a stable system, but today, within the context of the Social Age, *learning is a dynamic part of a dynamic system*, and we must adapt to fit the times, and not just with regard to the modes of delivery (mobile learning). Instead, our adaptation must be at the level of design, facilitation, assessment, and support. Organisations often worry more about the 'skills of the digital learner', when they should instead be concerned with the 'skills of the learning designer'.

Much of our older, formalised learning, was neither good nor effective. It was simply 'done'. It was abstract, and focused more on consistency, conformity, and replicability. In the Social Age, however, learning is increasingly dynamic, co-created, and adaptive, and it requires learners to become invested in the co-creation process.

Put simply, in the context of the Social Age, *we must develop new methodologies for learning*, and invest heavily in communities and Social Leaders who will deliver the new capabilities that we need. This is crucial, not only so that we may thrive, but also to avoid disruption and failure.

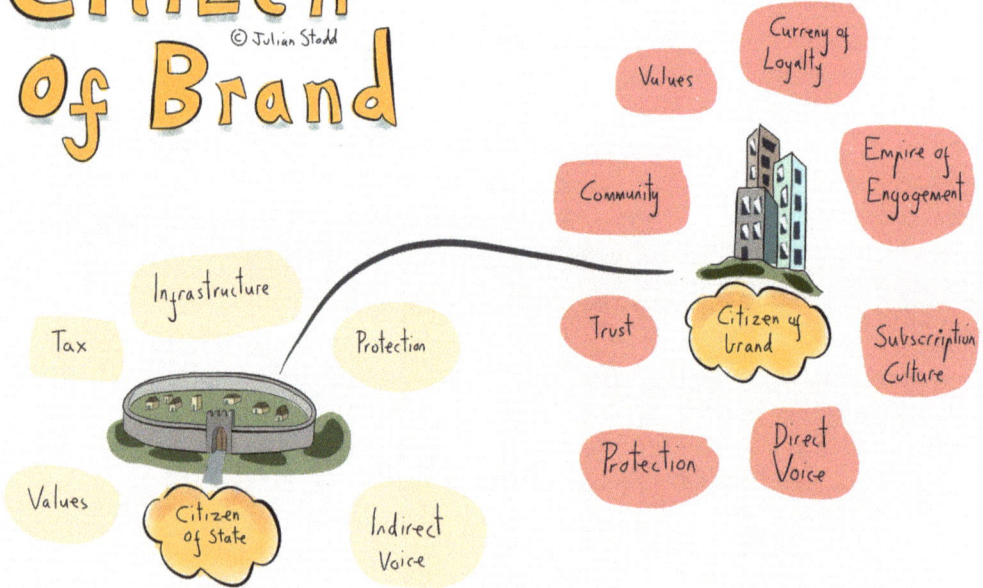

Citizen of Brand
© Julian Stodd

Values · Currency of Loyalty · Empire of Engagement · Community · Trust · Citizen of brand · Subscription Culture · Protection · Direct Voice

Tax · Infrastructure · Protection · Values · Citizen of State · Indirect Voice

THE NEW NATURE OF KNOWLEDGE

Semantics may kill us, but consider 'knowledge' itself – not on the deepest philosophical level, but on a rather mundane and practical one: Epistemology, or our most basic ways of knowing, are changing. We have moved from 'concentration' to 'distribution': Whereas we used to codify knowledge, and keep it in libraries, books, vaults, and experts (i.e. centralised, in 'centres of learning'), today it is dispersed, distributed, free – although, not without problems (validity, bias).

Clearly, we still need 'formal' knowledge, with its mechanisms of validation, replicability, and rigour. But the clear truth remains that, in many cases, we can do with 'just enough' knowledge to get us to the next step of the journey.

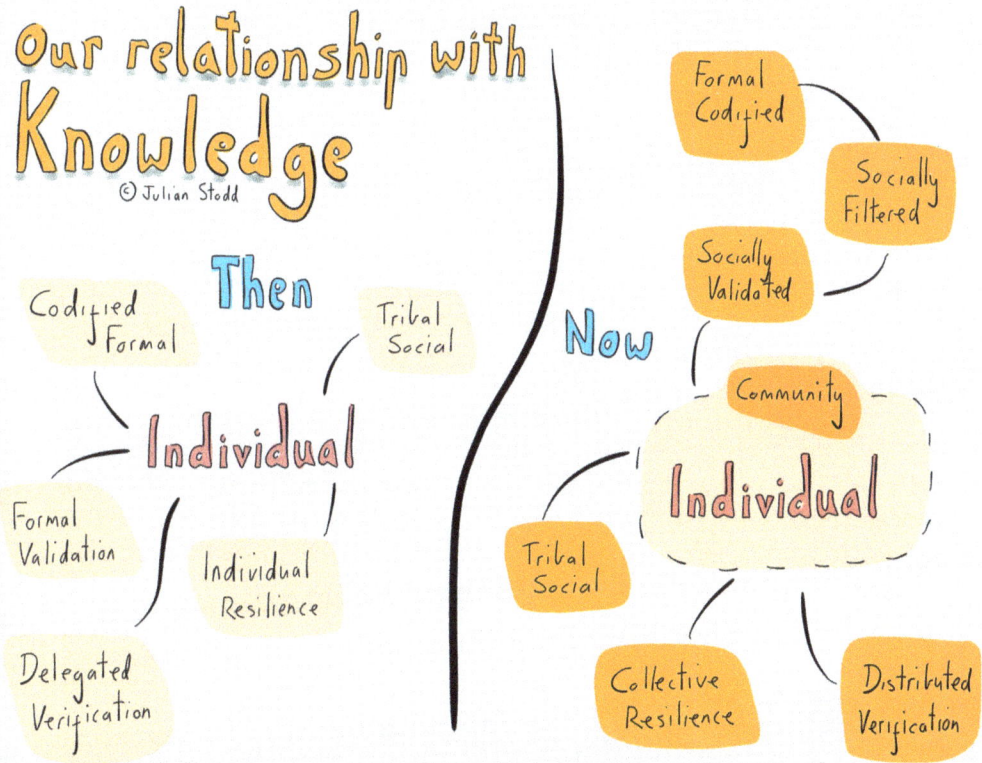

Our relationship with Knowledge
© Julian Stodd

Then

Codified Formal

Tribal Social

Individual

Formal Validation

Individual Resilience

Delegated Verification

Now

Formal Codified

Socially Filtered

Socially Validated

Community

Individual

Tribal Social

Collective Resilience

Distributed Verification

The knowledge that we codify and store may be perfect, but the knowledge that we access from our phone, whilst charging through an airport, to help us make a quick decision is pretty cool too. Is this type of distributed, community-moderated knowledge always right? Absolutely not. But to be fair, neither was all of our 'old' knowledge either. And, more importantly, *we are still creating the mechanisms of validation for social knowledge* that may make it ever better. This is a feature of the Social Age that is often misunderstood: What we see around us today is not the end state. Rather, it is often only an early prototype. Whilst broadly, the old system was static, the new one is constantly evolving, developing, and more importantly, improving.

Consider it like this: Our ecosystem of knowledge is diversified. We still need formal knowledge, with its checks and balances, but we also need social knowledge, with its accessibility and rapid evolution.

However, when it comes to knowledge, it's not just what we access that counts; There is a growing concern about the validity and value of that which we create. Can communities really create the quality of knowledge that we need?

Here again, we require pragmatic solutions. While people have commonly relied on local knowledge, and never had the access to question it, today this local tribal knowledge is liberated, to fly (be it good or bad) at scale. Perhaps, the best approach is this: If we worry about validity to the point where we take no action, then we cannot benefit from Social Learning. Conversely, if we liberate Social Learning with no consideration for the risks, we will ignite from the amount of risk we take on. So, we must learn how to do so in a way that is safe enough, but not dangerously safe.

The best way forward is to *create safe spaces*, to prototype, to experiment, to learn what really works within our own context. '*Experimentation*' is at the core of the Social Learning experience, and it's through this experimentation that we will learn new things that will help us evolve. *An organisation's ability to prototype, evolve, and cast off the old will differentiate it.*

However, a word of caution: In recent research, in a healthcare setting, we asked learners which technologies they used to collaborate. They identified seventeen different technologies, only one of which was sanctioned for use. Only one of which was permitted. Knowledge has already flown the coop: Denying the change will not prevent it. Instead, we must engage, to help the rapidly evolving social system to do better.

FORMAL & SOCIAL SYSTEMS: DYNAMIC TENSION

The formal system is everything that you can see, own, and control. Formal systems are where we create formal learning, and they are extremely good at, for example, collectivism, consistency, and achieving effect at scale (building Organisations that function globally).

The Dynamic
© Julian Stodd
Tension

Formal
Structure

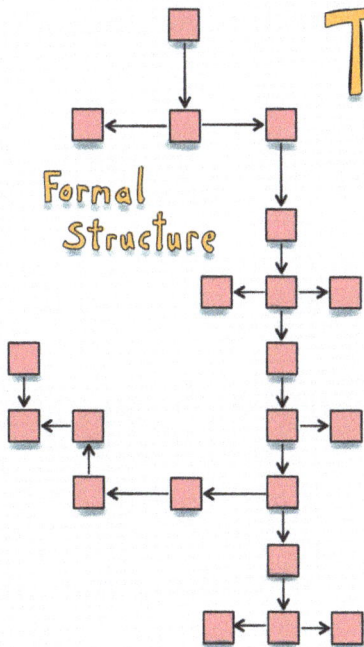

Social
Structure

Flowing around, and through, the formal system, are social systems. These are held, not in contractual relationships, but trust-based ones. Indeed, Social Systems are multi-layered, contextual, often internally conflicted, and ever-changing. Social systems are good at certain things that formal ones are unable to achieve: They are good at creative dissent, gentle subversion of outdated processes, questioning the system, radical creativity, social amplification, movement, momentum, curiosity, and innovation.

A modern organisation exists in a '*Dynamic Tension*' between the two, and Social Learning occurs at this intersection: Parts are formal and parts are social. Our challenge is to maintain, not deny or destroy, this tension [Stodd, 2017].

If the formal system triumphs, we achieve greater consistency, but we may not experience true learning, since we only learn what the formal organisation agrees with. If the social system wins, and completely subverts the formal structure, we lose our ability to formally validate quality, have consistency, and achieve global effect at scale. However, if we can master both (formal structure and social creativity held in a dynamic tension) we can thrive.

DEMOCRATISATION AND CONNECTIVITY

The Social Age has seen the broad democratisation of a range of things: storytelling, communication, innovation, creativity, research, even power itself.

This democratisation (moving ownership and control away from formal structures) is not purely a function of emergent social technologies and an evolved sociology;

6 The future for Organisations lies in learning to become **Socially Dynamic**

© Julian Stodd

1 The **Social Age** provides the new context in which our organisations are grounded.

5 Carrying great formal and Social strength within a **Dynamic Tension**

Social Leaders find power outside the system. They help us find balance and momentum

2 It's an **Evolved** structure of **Power**, rebalanced between formal and social systems.

4 It's not just change within a known space, but rather our work, our challenge is to **Build a new** system.

3 We must consider **Systemic Change** in depth, throughout our Organisations

It's also a function of the failure of existing systems to adapt. The rise of MOOCs could be seen as an emergent threat to existing education providers, but they are complicit in that rise. Had universities spent less time and effort protecting existing revenue streams, and not remained so wedded to the geolocation of learning, they could have innovated in this space themselves.

Connectivity also represents a fundamental social shift: Whilst our strong social ties used to be based on a shared language, increasingly they are able to be broadly distributed and, with the imminent proliferation of synchronous machine translation, culturally diverse. *We are substantially liberated from language, time, and place.* Hence, the structures of formal power that grew within those old spaces have begun to lose relevance, unless they adapt. Translation is not simply the transliteration of words: It enables the transculturation of ideas too, of ways of knowing.

Authority within formal systems is represented by rank, title, and formal qualification. In social systems, authority is granted by the system, and based on reputation, trust, fairness, and the investments we make over time. It's this Social Authority that we draw upon within learning communities: It's your reputation that counts.

So, in the context of Social Learning, our ability to learn (collaboratively and socially), depends partly on our Social Authority, and our level of Social Capital; As much as we need political skills to thrive in formal spaces, so we need social skills to thrive in social ones. Indeed, we need to consider this when determining how to create the most effective conditions for Social Learning. We must also figure out how to embed the necessary skills and capabilities to support every community member.

SUMMARY

The Social Age is our current evolved reality, and it is the new context of learning.

WHAT YOU NEED TO KNOW:

- *Formal and social systems exist within a Dynamic Tension that we should seek to maintain.*

- *The underlying power has shifted, and with this change, new relationships are created between the learner and the socially moderated authority.*

- *Knowledge is increasingly distributed, decentralised, co-created.*

WHAT YOU NEED TO DO:

- *Find ways to recognise and empower Social Authority within your organisation: consider the spaces and mechanisms by which you will enable dialogue between the two powers.*

- *Consider how well you have established your Learning function, as it moves from providing learning, to enabling it: consider new roles and evolve old ones.*

- *Recognise that old models of validating your 'known knowledge' may be outdated: consider how you will revise them.*

NOTES

SCAFFOLDED SOCIAL LEARNING

Let's consider a design approach for Social Learning – a methodology that we can apply to the design, delivery, facilitation, and support of this type of co-creative learning.

Stodd [2014] has proposed the Scaffolded Social Learning model: a design approach that defines a series of co-creative spaces, formal learning assets, gateways, and the learning community, to help you initiate Social Learning in an organisational context.

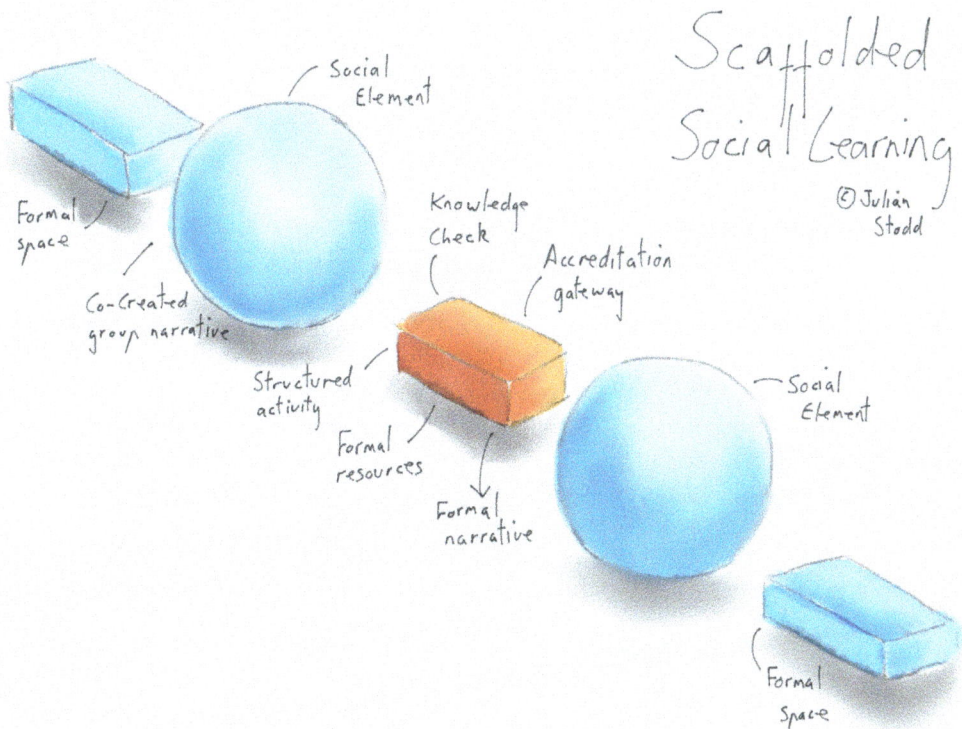

A DESIGN APPROACH

A Social Learning journey will see the learner engage with formal assets (stories written by the organisation, codified and accepted knowledge), social assets (tribal, tacit, knowledge held within the community), and individual knowledge (worldview, preconceptions, bias, existing knowledge). From a design perspective, we can vary the amount of formal knowledge we input, we can create conditions where tribal knowledge will be shared, and we can create reflective opportunities for people to explore their own preconceived knowledge.

The 'Scaffolding' in Scaffolded Social Learning represents the structure that both carries us forward with momentum, and also the structure of the three types of knowledge with which we interact. The Scaffolding can also determine specific activities and opportunities to manipulate the data (i.e. to 'make sense' of it all) both individually for each learner and collectively as a group.

Another key difference between formal learning and Social Learning is that 'formal' is always and inherently, abstract, whilst 'social' is inherently applied, because it occurs in your everyday reality.

Conversely, formal learning often occurs in special spaces.

Moreover, a well-designed Scaffolded Social Learning experience will contain differentiated 'Learning', 'Rehearsal', and 'Performance' spaces.

On a technical level, the design of Scaffolded Learning involves choreographing the entire experience: i.e. creating each of these three spaces. Typically, like a good play, the learning occurs in a 'Running Order', which determines which formal assets are released at which times, what stage the community is at, and the sequencing of the storytelling, which we will discuss more later. Also like a play, it involves a range of supporting roles, both on stage and behind-the-scenes (community managers, storytellers, coaches, Social Leaders).

Thus, Scaffolded Social Learning brings together the best of formal approaches (the story that the organisation tells) and the best of the socially co-created ones (the tribal narrative).

It defines a series of co-created spaces, within which we utilise specific co-creative behaviours to both provoke and support the manipulation and processing of new knowledge, and further create spaces in which people can demonstrate their own specific expertise.

The gateways ensure that we maintain momentum, and they may be used to either create scarcity or bestow honour to increase engagement.

CO-CREATIVE BEHAVIOURS

We can define and utilise specific co-creative behaviours to enrich community activities. This technique is about putting loose structure into conversations and creating common patterns of activity which allow us to draw narrative threads between the stories.

One example of a co-creative behaviour is '*curation*': In Scaffolded Social Learning, we might encourage other learners to bring in their own formal examples, rather than do so ourselves. Instead of me saying, '*Here is a great example of Social Learning in action*', I would invite you to curate an example.

Now, you may give an example that seems terrible to me, and I may give one that seems way off track to you – thus, another co-creative behaviour should come into play, i.e. '*Interpretation*'. In interpretation, I write a narrative about why i think the case study I have provided as an example is relevant. So, you tell your story (interpreting the thing you curated) and I tell mine.

Will we agree? Well, that doesn't matter: Social Learning is not about conformity and agreement, it's about broadening one's understanding, context, and perspective. Thus, I cannot deny the validity of your example, although I am absolutely allowed to challenge it and engage in a debate about it. Indeed, '*challenge*' is another co-creative behaviour.

Much of what we are doing in the design of the Scaffolding concerns moving the '*location*' of stories: I tell a story, you respond, I try to tell your story, you respond, and we both collaborate to respond to a third story. In this way, we all come together to co-create an overall narrative.

Will our story be right? Well, '*right*' is subjective. If you teach me how to change the carburettor on my car (good luck…), then am I '*right*' if I do it exactly like you do it, or am I 'right' if my car starts again, even if I did something different?

For example, when I was younger I was reprimanded for a poem I had to write at school: It was not good enough, I was told. But by what right can the teacher tell me that my poem is not good, when a poem is a matter of self-expression? Almost by definition, any poem that I write is as good as what anyone else writes. Unless by '*right*', we mean '*conforms*'. My poem may not have conformed, but it was still '*right*' for me.

Our ability as Social Learning designers is largely connected to our ability to define, and master, the usage, combination, and creativity, of our co-creative approaches, and to use them to craft both engaging and effective spaces in which to learn together.

ASSESSMENT

Assessment is a common concern in Social Learning, so it's worth saying at the start that you can measure Social Learning as effectively as you can measure formal learning, although with the caveat that this is really not saying much.
Often, in the assessment of formal learning we are measuring knowledge, and not necessarily application.

In general, *it's worth triangulating approaches for the measurement of Social Learning*: For example, do you, as a learner, feel that you have learned? Does your community believe that you are learning? Do you score more highly in a formal test of knowledge or a simulation-based assessment of capability? Triangulating between a range of these measures gives us our best route to success: How I feel about what I have learned (i.e. my personal narrative of learning and change over time) combined with how others see me learning and changing, in addition to my individual ability to demonstrate what I have learned and apply it is a much better measure of achievement.

[If you are particularly interested in Assessment, there is a chapter in my book on Learning Methodology dedicated to this]

MEASUREMENT

As my old professor once said, 'You can measure everything'. However, a pertinent follow-up question may be, 'But what are you going to do with it?'.

The technology we are likely using to deploy Social Learning comes with the convenient attribute of measurement: Many systems discuss 'engagement' with regard to 'clicking' or 'interaction'. Technology certainly allows us to measure quite a bit, but we need to consider what we will measure, how we will measure it, and what we will do as a result. Unless we can answer all three of these questions clearly, it's best not to measure at all.

The challenge of 'measurement' is often used to attack the concept of Social Learning, as though it doesn't apply to all other forms of learning as well. A more valuable question to ask may be, 'What on earth have we spent our time measuring before' or even, 'What can we stop measuring now'. Measurement is enticing, but not always of value.

Instead, we should focus on outcomes, and triangulate between self-assessed methods of measurement, observational ones, and formally moderated ones. But never be afraid to ask the question, 'What if we didn't measure at all?'.

SPACE, PERMISSION, AND CONSEQUENCE

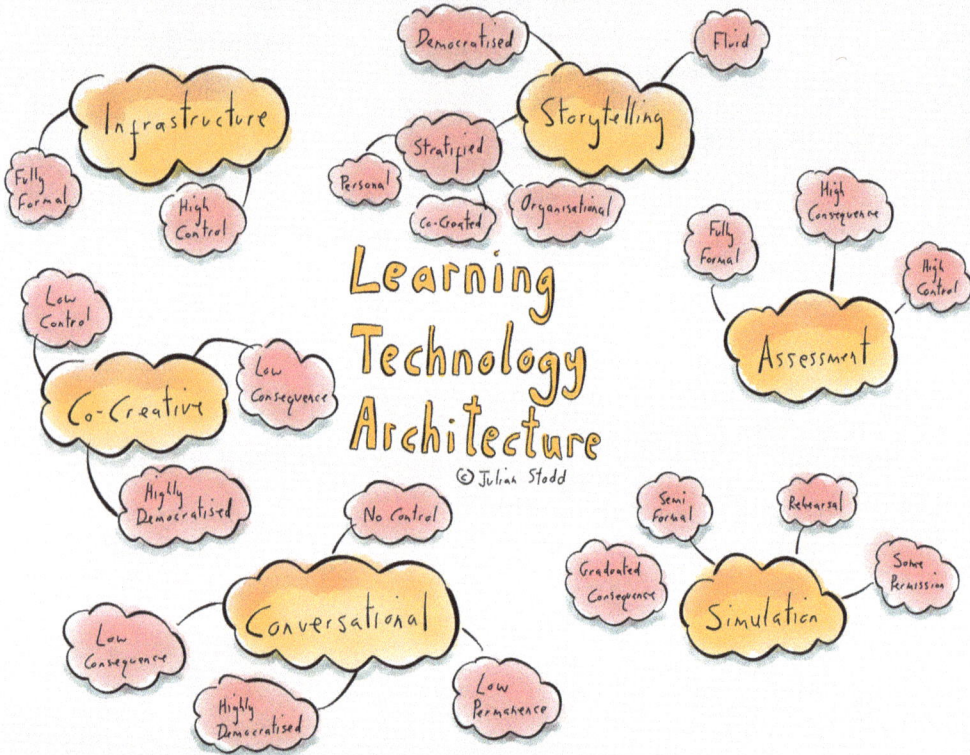

At the heart of Social Learning is the learning space. This is the place where we come together to participate in the central 'sense making' activity. Or, perhaps I should say 'spaces', because one thing is very clear: 'Space' is very different from 'community', and 'permission' is something just as easily claimed, as it is awarded. An understanding of how we create the right kind of spaces, embrace and build coherent and effective communities, and ensure that permission is clear, is vital to really understand Social Learning.

The analogy most commonly used to describe 'space' and 'community' is that of building a new town: You can build houses, a mall, a church, and a town square; you can landscape the gardens; You can move people into those houses; but you won't necessarily have a community.

To Explore — Perspectives   Skills — To Rehearse

Ideas   Differences   Conversations   Behaviours

With Technology

Hold Open Spaces

© Julian Stodd

For Community

Structure   Approaches   Surplus   Ideas

To Innovate — Workflow   Uncertainty   To Share

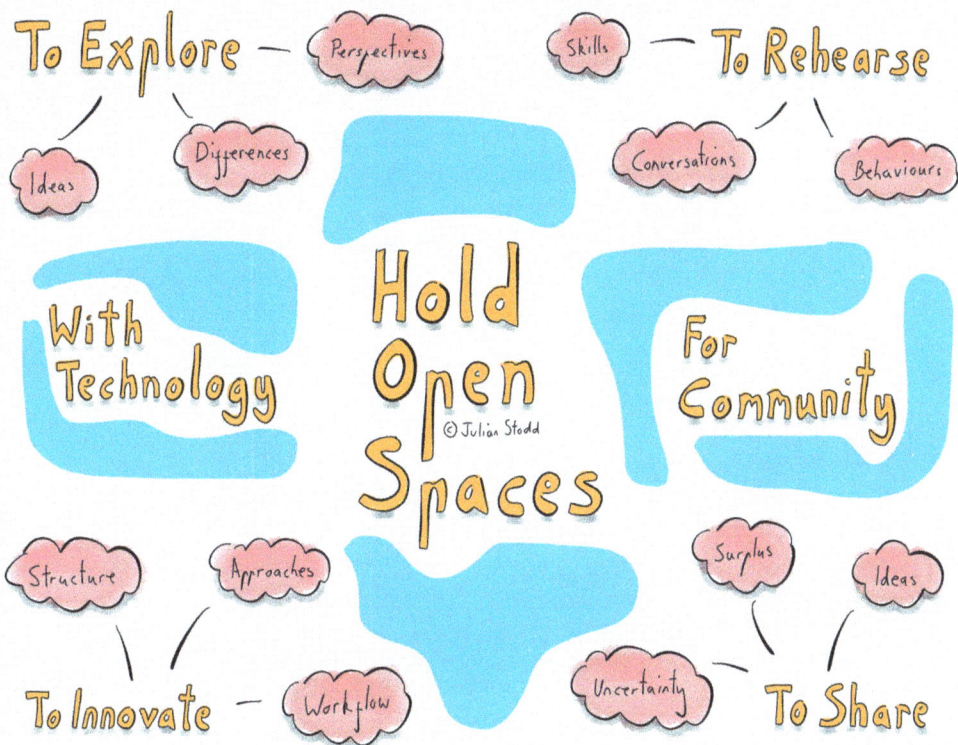

It's when two of those people come together, on a street corner, and have a conversation about what a terrible job you've done on the brickwork. That's when you have the seeds of community.

The buildings form the space, but the conversation is the foundation of the community. And conversations can move between multiple spaces.

When we provide space for Social Learning, be that a classroom, a chat room, or some kind of Learning Management System, we should be fully aware that we have not built a community. Registering users, giving them avatars, even a fully immersive simulation environment, that is not a community.

In fact, the learners probably exist in a community across multiple spaces and even multiple technologies: Conversations start in one space, and gradually move to another. We favour a model of technology for learning that takes this into account. Where are the conversational spaces? Where are the collaborative spaces? Where are the core infrastructure spaces (where we provide the formal components)? Where are the subversive spaces? Where are the assessment spaces?

You'll see in the diagram that each is differentiated by notions of '*permanence*' and '*consequence*'. Spaces should be graded; For example, a conversational space requires a high degree of impermanence, whilst a formal assessment space may require exactly the opposite. Collaboration spaces should be low consequence, whilst performance spaces may be high consequence.

In reality, Social Learning takes place within a diverse ecosystem of technology, and the ability to construct such a space is a core skill for a Socially Dynamic Organisation.

Nevertheless, engagement is not simply a function of technology and consequence. Other factors significantly impact engagement. For example, ownership of the rules can drive engagement: whether the rules are applied by the organisation or whether the community is allowed to write, or co-write, the rules. When allowed to contribute to the rules, engagement within a community typically increases.

In most contexts, learners organise rapidly and diversify their own ecosystem of technology; For example, they 'meet' in the formal space, but rapidly establish personal connections on Facebook, chat on WhatsApp, build connectivity on LinkedIn, establish personal email connections, and so on. We tend to build redundancy into our network within these social spaces, and we expect consequence to apply accordingly.

In formal spaces, we understand that consequence is owned by the organisation itself. But in social ones, who owns consequence?

There are two answers: first, a formal or even legal one, and second, a social one. *If we apply formal power and consequence within social spaces, we simply make them formal.* Going in with a heavy hand and applying consequence tends to drive down engagement or, worse, completely drives out diversity of expressed opinions. In social spaces, it is important to tread carefully with formal power. Moreover, remember that engagement is something that we earn, not something that we demand.

SUMMARY

Scaffolded Social Learning is a design methodology that allows us to balance formal assets, socially created assets, and the existing knowledge and understanding of each individual learner.

WHAT YOU NEED TO KNOW:

- *The 'learning' in Social Learning does not just happen on your Learning Management System: We inhabit a diverse ecosystem of collaborative technologies, and conversations move between them.*

- *We can use specific co-creative behaviours within the Scaffolding to encourage interaction and create common outputs.*

- *Measurement and assessment are vital, but we need to ensure that what we are measuring is actionable.*

WHAT YOU NEED TO DO:

- *Identify the skills gap in your current learning team: focus on choreography, Scaffolding, facilitation, storytelling, and measurement, then create experimental spaces in which everyone can learn and rehearse these skills.*

- *Enhance your co-creative behaviours and develop your capability in using them.*

- *Map your spaces: determine which are formal and which social; consider the ways you share that knowledge and understand different views.*

NOTES

SOCIAL LEARNING COMMUNITIES

At the heart of Social Learning are our learning communities. In this section, we'll explore what learning communities are, and how we can create the optimum conditions for them to thrive.

In our own work at Sea Salt Learning, we have found that it pays to dedicate time to first establishing the community, before moving onto any formal learning activity. Before you can be purposeful, you need to be coherent. We use the term '*coherent*', in this case, to describe an established, high-functioning community.

Strong Social Leadership · Broad Fairness · Equal Opportunity · Trust · Need · Clarity of Consequence · Fluidity of Role · Clear Rules · Purpose · Democratised Space · Shared Values · High Social Capital · Segmented Utility

Conditions for Community

© Julian Stodd

SENSE-MAKING ENTITIES

Coherent communities are 'sense-making' entities: They help us figure out what is right, what is wrong, what is valuable, and what to do about any of it. *Our social communities help us filter out noise and notice signals*, and also to understand these signals.

Within the context of Social Learning, where much of the 'sense-making' is done in the community, this 'sense making' mitigates for diversifying the people within it: The more diverse the community is with regard to worldview, experience, cultural profile, and capability, the more effective we all are.

The rise of Social Communities is a core aspect of the new ecosystem of the Social Age. Facilitated by technology and fundamentally about people, these Social Communities are claiming power in opposition to formal systems in every area.

MECHANISMS OF ENGAGEMENT

When we surveyed a group of UK NHS professionals about how they found their most valuable learning communities, they responded that they had been invited. Many of our communities are hidden, not advertised on job boards. And the mechanisms by which we engage in them are extremely important.

Within the formal system, we are assigned roles by the organisation, but in Social Systems our roles are more fluid, and they change more often. Sometimes we bring specific expertise, resources, or capabilities, and sometimes we bring challenges or support; sometimes we are cross connectors, a link between the different communities, and sometimes we simply come to learn. When considering Social Learning communities, it's worth remembering that *we do not need to get everyone to engage in a certain way: We just need broad engagement.* It's fine, desirable even, for people to take diversified roles.

Community

Nurture · Support · Lead · Facilitate · Your Role · Engage · Grow · Moderate · Narrate · Crossover

© Julian Stodd

RITUALS AND CHOREOGRAPHY

Reciprocity

Recognition

Meaning

Artefacts

Rituals

Contextual

Identity

Gifts

Investment

Control

Generosity

Unifying

Trust

Community

Kindness

Tokens

Divisive

Tribal

© Julian Stodd

There is a role for ritual: In our own research, people described the 'rituals of welcome and engagement' as the single most important factor for their future success within a community. The way in which we are welcomed into a community counts. Also, Ritual is something within our control; Indeed, when designing the Scaffolding for learning, we can actively write our own ritual or consciously adopt existing rituals.

For example, we can work with community members on their rituals of engagement for new members, and we can work with their formal managers on the rituals they will use when the learners share their stories with the rest of their team. In one organisation, we worked with the managers to help them create a ritual where, when people came back from courses, they were thanked for taking time away from work to learn, and the managers even created structured spaces for them in which to share their learning.

This is all part of the choreography of learning: the end-to-end experience, which is how we should consider learning design in the Social Age. In much of our broader life and experience, we are seeing a shift from 'transaction' to 'experience', and learning is no different.

We should be crafting learning journeys and experiences that focus on end-to-end engagement. This means that we need to pay equal attention to every part of the learning experience: the email that invites someone to join, the instructions they receive to register, the way we thank them for sharing their stories, how they graduate at the end. Each part should be carefully scripted and crafted according to your specific running order.

Together, rituals and choreography form a powerful tool for community building and learning engagement. Even simple things like artefacts (by including others in their creation and giving them out as awards) can be powerful. In our own work, the artefacts that the learners and communities create have been many and varied: One group created '*gratitude stones*', which the group awarded to those who they felt had helped them to succeed the most. These items have no financial value; They are merely honorific goods, but it is precisely that honorific value that makes them effective. No plastic trinkets here, but rather rituals of gratitude and artefacts of value which, coincidentally, are exactly the things we use in our 'real' lives (birthday cards, thank you cards, celebratory songs – all of these are things that carry no financial value, but express deep sentiment).

HIDDEN COMMUNITIES

We will never locate all of the communities within an organisation: Some (like our learning communities) are visible and formally sanctioned, whilst others exist outside our network and experience. Some exist in active opposition, deliberately hidden from us.

When we ask people what their most valuable communities are for learning, they often speak of hidden communities: WhatsApp groups, Facebook groups, places which exist beyond formal oversight and consequence.

It's worth remembering that these are not a new feature: We have always existed within a web of communities, ranging from fully social to fully formal. However, within the context of the Social Age, the boundaries between the two have become fully blurred, and whilst formal communities have not encroached beyond the organisation, social ones have fully invaded that previously sacrosanct space.

The difference today is that these communities, these hidden communities, can form and operate at an incredible scale, and do so right under our noses. This is the consequence of the democratisation of communication and connectivity.

SANCTIONED SUBVERSION

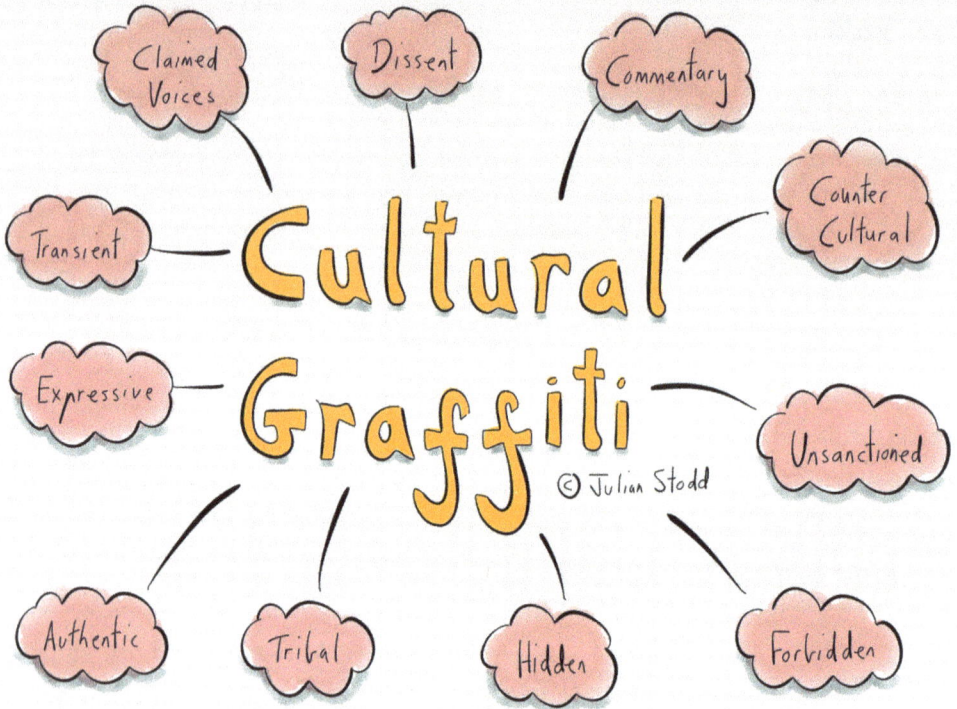

Claimed Voices

Dissent

Commentary

Transient

Counter Cultural

Cultural Graffiti
© Julian Stodd

Expressive

Unsanctioned

Authentic

Tribal

Hidden

Forbidden

Moving ourselves beyond a binary understanding of which answers are 'right' or 'wrong' is valuable. Sometimes, the answer lies in breaking open the question. Subversion itself can be of great benefit to formal systems, if they are willing to listen, because they are typically inadequate at subverting (or evolving) themselves.

Consider this: How many organisations put as much time, energy, and effort into deconstructing redundant processes and un-writing outdated rules, as they do into forming them in the first place. Very few! So, what happens as a result of this organisational detritus? Typically, it's subverted: People work around redundant systems and sub-optimised processes. And they do so not only individually, but collectively as well. Indeed, when we join a new organisation, much of what we learn, on a local, tribal level, in the early days of our engagement, is exactly this type of crowd-sourced subversion.

However, it is not expressed as such: it's usually held under the generic banner of 'how we get things done around here'. But that 'around here' mentality generally reflects the ways that we optimise, on a local level, quite often by ignoring superfluous formal rules.

And here's the thing, there is great value in listening to and learning from all of this, because **rules do not give you excellence**. Excellence exists in people, and if we are willing to listen to this subversive experience, we can learn from it.

Consider compliance for a moment. No organisation is fully compliant, no matter how many rules it writes, because compliance is not a function of rules. Rather, it's a feature of culture. If you have a healthy culture, non-compliance is almost unthinkable. Rules set boundaries, but individual behaviour is what gives us excellence. Create space for people to dissent, sanctioned spaces for subversion, and when you hear of rule-breaking, rather than punish, try to learn. Instead, thank those people for helping make the organisation better.

SUMMARY

WHAT YOU NEED TO KNOW:

- *Communities are 'sense-making' entities, and as such, form a vital part of our distributed capability apparatus. We must nurture and support them...*

- *...but we do not own them, and many exist beyond our oversight, visibility, or control.*

- *There is value in understanding the role and power of rituals, and how artefacts can be valued beyond simple monetary means.*

WHAT YOU NEED TO DO:

- *Experiment with rituals: try documenting the ones you see around you, and try writing and rehearsing some specific ones of your own; relate them to engagement in Social Learning.*

- *Consider allowing the group to define their own rewards e.g. let them name and validate it, then award it.*

- *Consider how you can support and empower, not only the visible and sanctioned communities, but thet hidden ones as well. Offer time, resources, space, and acknowledgement.*

NOTES

STORYTELLING IN SOCIAL LEARNING

Stories are at the core of Social Learning: the formal stories that we share in a community, the co-created stories written by learners in their 'sense-making' activities, and the personal narratives of learning and change over time, which form the legacy of the journey.

Each of these types of story brings different value. Personal Stories cannot be disputed, they are both part of the evolution of our worldview and the narrative of it. Personal stories are typically highly authentic, and hence much loved by the community.

How We Can Use Stories

In an agile organisation this is based on the personal and co-created stories

A personal narrative of learning over time

The co-created and co-owned story written by a community

© Julian Stodd

organisation

Personal

Co-Created

Co-Created Stories are not always stories of consensus, but may be a chance to document our differences, which is exactly how it should be. Learning is not about conformity and consensus, it's about creative differences and constructive dissent. We need broad capability as an output, not broad conformity. Indeed, the monocultural cognition of an identikit organisation may be the antithesis of the agility we need to face the challenges and changes of the Social Age.

Organisations are used to writing Organisational Stories, or monolithic narratives, which they push out into the system, but as they become more Socially Dynamic, they need to learn to write stories that are an aggregate of both personal and co-created narratives. In other words, the organisational view of learning should at least partly reflect and value the views held by the community, and not simply try to colonise or control them.

There are a range of specific techniques that you can use in storytelling for Social Learning, such as 'Diagonal Storytelling', in which communities cut through the layers of formal hierarchy and collaborate to produce a story with multiple perspectives. This technique creates 'Stories of Difference', in which learners document, in detail, the sheer breadth of their disagreement. Engaging in stories of difference is a valuable way to counter the echo chamber of conformity. Engaging in storytelling spaces, and community spaces for that matter, where we disagree is a great way to diversify the 'sense-making'.

Often, we find that organisations, as they plan for Social Learning, worry about engagement. How will they entice people to share the first stories? However, they should be worrying more about Story Listening: How will they respond when they hear stories that they do not like?

Story
Hearing
Spaces · Permission · Power · Trust · Consequence

Listening
© Julian Stodd

Access · Validity · Currency

ThanKing · Influence · Diversity · Respecting

Dissent

Visibility · Timeliness · Responding · Difference · Viewpoint

This is the challenge: If you want to feel safe (not 'be' safe mind you, safety is largely a delusion), then stick with formal learning, and assess people as 'ready' if they tell you what you want to hear. Social Learning, on the contrary, is about creative dissent, sanctioned subversion, and real, cold, hard, performance. It's a type of learning that builds real capability, but only if we are willing to listen.

That's the ultimate irony: The organisation that adopts Social Learning may believe that it is helping people learn differently, but often, if done right, it is the organisation itself that does most of the learning.

We need to actively consider how we listen, how and when we moderate, and how we respond.

Giving communities time to self-moderate is generally more valuable than trying to control the conversation. After all, Learning Communities are not the final answer. Rather, they are the working spaces where we learn the final answer. And as such, they need space to operate, and the permission (claimed, or granted) to be wrong along the way. Or, they need to convince us that the answer we think is wrong is actually right…

OWNERSHIP AND CONTROL

But who owns the stories that are written? The question surrounding ownership is interesting for several reasons. Generally, people are very willing to invest both time and ideas into the community, if it is to the benefit of community. Indeed, when asked, people will typically say that the main thing they want to do is help others achieve. But, if the value created leads to direct financial gain for the organisation, people are more likely to demand financial reward, or their 'cut'. Thus, it is important to remember that the context of a conversation can directly relate to the desired reward. There is no 'one answer'; We need to, instead, build an understanding of how social and formal rewards 'work', and how we can best, and fluidly, apply them.

Broadly speaking, we cannot 'mark' the stories that are written as part of Social Learning, because that is like marking art. Even if you disagree, another's creative expression should never be invalidated. Similarly, my story is my story. You can like it, or not, it's still mine.

Instead, consider how we can bridge the gap between stories to better understand the similarities and differences. Again, broadly what we should be feeling and expressing is a gratitude that we are allowed to read them, and not be passing judgement upon them.

STORYTELLING IN SOCIAL LEARNING

The mindset that an organisation should bring to the table when discussing Social Learning is one of gratitude: the prizes of capability and resilience that it brings are not like gold lying around on the floor, waiting to be picked up.

If we want it, we must earn it, and invest in it. This is a better attitude for understanding every aspect, from the design of Scaffolded Social Learning, to the ways in which we empower individual learners, recognise and reward them, and even learn from the shared stories. We should aim to invest in co-creation, not demand it.

Social Leadership:
My First 100 days
by Julian Stodd

CALENDAR

Investing
in
Co - Creation

© Julian Stodd

TRIBES AND TRUST

The Landscape of Trust
© Julian Stodd

1. When we meet we project a frame

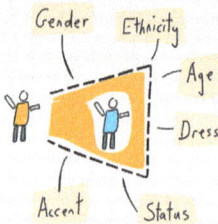

Gender   Ethnicity
— Age
— Dress
Accent   Status

2. We are influenced by cultural norms and bias

3. Subsequent actions validate or refute the frame

The Projection of Trust

4. Judgement is imposed as the implicit rules are met or breached

Trust Fails

5. Failure of trust may therefore be an imposed projection

If the natural order of the formal system is hierarchy, then the order of the social one is tribes: strong trust-bonded units, which aggregate up into wider communities and eventually, to the overarching organisation and into broader society.

I describe tribes as 'trust-bonded', because that is the clear context that emerges from the body of Landscape of Trust research. Indeed, people's trust in organisations is failing, and being rapidly replaced with trust in communities and tribes.

People overwhelmingly answer that trust fails due to 'the breaching of implicit rules'. Thus, one thing we can seek to do when establishing our communities, is to make the implicit, explicit: be clear about spaces and permission, be clear about the ownership and oversight of the conversations, and be clear about which rules apply, or the ways in which people can contribute to the rules.

Earning trust is hard, but the consequences of breaking it are harder. When trust fails, it seems to fail hard, fragmenting culture to the point where Social Learning becomes all but a distant dream.

SUMMARY

WHAT YOU NEED TO KNOW:

- In Social Learning, we can consider three levels of narrative: personal, co-created, and organisational. Find ways to join the three.

- You don't own the stories that are written within the walls of the organisation: you need to consider how ownership is determined, fairly.

- Tribes are trust-bonded structures, but we should not assume that people 'trust' the organisation itself. Trust is earned, and engagement is a function of trust.

WHAT YOU NEED TO DO:

- Map out your story ecosystem: Where do formal stories live? Where are the co-created ones? Where do you share personal stories? Create, and support, an institutional story space where you can 'hear' all three.

- Whenever you broadcast a story, be explicit about where the space for response exists, and learn to story listen.

- Work with senior leaders to answer the question, 'How will we invest in co-creation'. Consider mechanisms of reputation based on reward and opportunity.

NOTES

A SOCIAL LEARNING CULTURE

We've covered a lot of ground, so let's summarise where we have got to:

- *Learning is changing:* *Against the backdrop of the Social Age, the type of knowledge we engage with everyday has changed: It is often co-created, geo-located, adaptive, and hidden within our social communities.*

- *Scaffolded Social Learning is a design methodology* *that creates a loose structure – a scaffolding if you will – within which learning communities participate in 'sense-making' activities, while simultaneously engaging with both formal and socially-gifted knowledge.*

- *Learning takes place within communities that exist outside of formal structures; These new spaces are trust-bonded, complex, and powerful.* *Our challenge is to create the necessary conditions for communities to thrive.*

- *Within these communities, learners create stories and produce narratives (both individually, and collectively). These stories can inform the wider organisation,* *if it has the humility, and willingness, to learn.*

- *But, we should handle such stories with care. Adopting* *Social Learning is just one part of a wider cultural transformation, and it's a transformation that may break the established wisdom, and established power, of every other part of the organisation.*

Stories, communities, and learning are all expressions of power. And, as we've learned, within the context of the Social Age, power is evolving.

As we engage in Social Learning, we will discover that our formal power is irrelevant in social spaces. Within these new learning communities, you can shout all you like, but it's Social Authority (i.e. reputation-based influence) which counts the most. So, in the course of adopting Social Learning, we inadvertently erode the power of the formal organisation.

As we empower the social community, this newly empowered community will demand greater freedom and power.

If our aim is learning transformation, then this power is what will drive the change. But it's a champagne bottle to uncork with all the inherent risk: loss of formal power, loss of formal control, in return for social engagement, enhanced sense making, stronger trust, and high engagement.

The tension between formal systems of control and socially moderated systems, is a Dynamic Tension which should only be upset with care.

A Socially Dynamic Organisation will find a new balance: the very best of the formal (system, process, hierarchy, and control) combined with the very best of the Social (creativity, subversion, innovation, and amplification).

This is our challenge: To craft more collaborative models of learning, and to learn how to build an organisational culture in which learning can thrive.

OTHER RESOURCES, AND OFFERINGS

I share all my work openly, through the blog, through my ten books, and nearly 2,000 articles. Here are a selection of other resources and offerings.

THE GUIDEBOOK SERIES

I've written a series of *'Guidebooks'* for the Social Age: these cover aspects of my work that are still rapidly evolving, or which I have not made time to write a full book about yet. They are typically under 10k words, and are intended to provide an overview of the landscape. I try to keep them practical, with a key highlight on *'what you need to know'*, and *'what you can do about it'*.

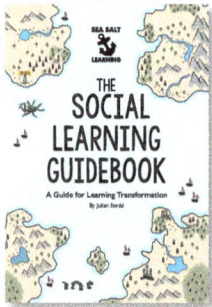

The Social Learning Guidebook

Provides a practical overview for the principles and design techniques of Social Learning in a modern organisation.

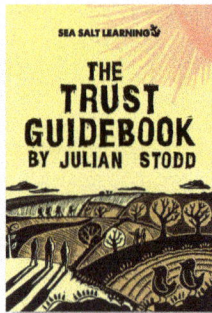

The Trust Guidebook

Explores our extensive research into the Landscape of Trust, and asks 72 questions that leaders can use with their teams.

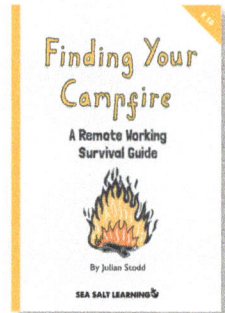

Finding Your Campfire

This short book is a survival guide for individuals, teams, and organisations navigating the experience of remote work.

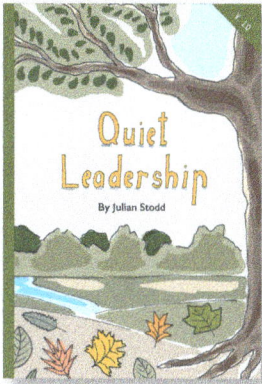

Quiet Leadership considers the Organisations that we inhabit as an ecosystem, and the way that none of us can tend to the whole of this system alone. Only by connecting at the most local level, through the smallest of actions, can we weave a strength into our culture, and keep the ecosystem healthy at scale.

The Humble Leader is a guided reflection into our personal humility as a Social Leader.

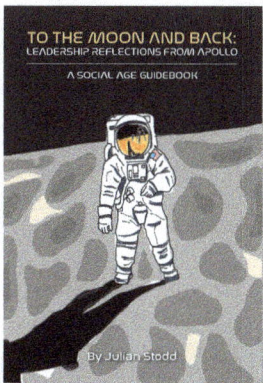

To the Moon and Back: Leadership Reflections from Apollo shares eight key stories about the Apollo programme, alongside my personal reflection on what this means for Leadership in the Social Age.

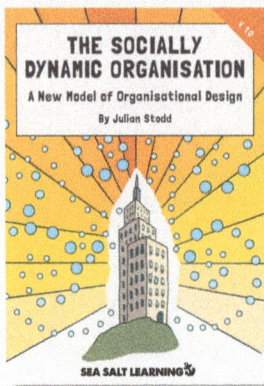

The Socially Dynamic Organisation
For a new type of world, we will need a new type of Organisation: one that is lightweight and rapidly adaptable, that thrives in times of constant change, that respects the old but embraces the new.

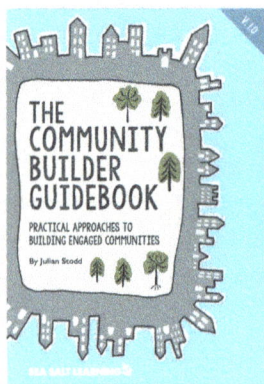

The Community Builder Guidebook
brings you practical ideas to create engaged and dynamic Social Learning Communities and Communities of Practice.

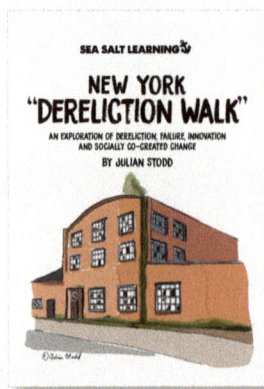

The New York Dereliction Walk is more experimental work, exploring how Organisations and ideas fall derelict and fail, but can be reborn through social movements. It was my favourite writing from 2018.

THE HANDBOOK SERIES

'Handbooks' are intended to capture a full snapshot of my evolving body of work on a particular subject. 'The Social Leadership Handbook', now in its second edition, explores the intersection of Formal and Social authority, and considers the importance of this in the context of the Social Age.

I'm currently finishing writing 'The Change Handbook', which is an exploration of how Organisations change, and the forces that hold them constrained. It considers how we build more Socially Dynamic Organisations.

THE '100 DAY', & 'SKETCHBOOK', SERIES

Whilst *'Handbooks'* and *'Guidebooks'* are about ideas and strategy, the *'100 Day'* books tackle how we do these things at scale. They do so by providing a scaffolded space, which you can explore, document, and graffiti, as you go.

'Social Leadership: My First 100 Days' is a practical, guided, reflective journey. It follows 100 days of activity, with each day including provocations, questions, and actions. You fill in the book as you go. It's accompanied by a full set of 100 podcasts.

'The Trust Sketchbook' is another guided, reflective journey, a walk through the Landscape of Trust, but in this case you graffiti and adapt the book, to capture your own landscape.

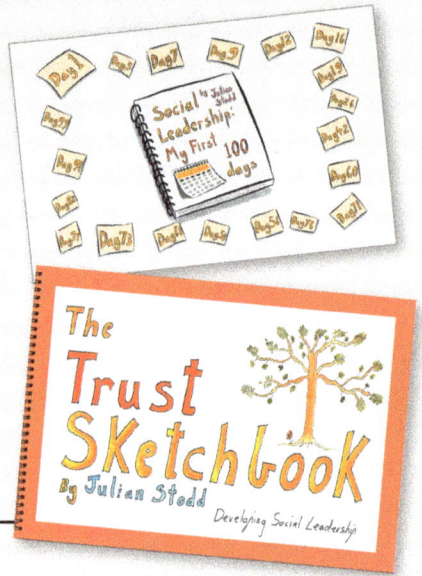

OTHER BOOKS

I have written a series of other books, covering aspects of learning, culture technology, and knowledge, which you can find details of on the blog.

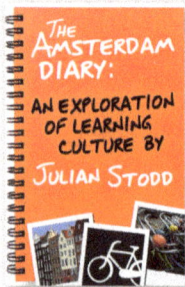

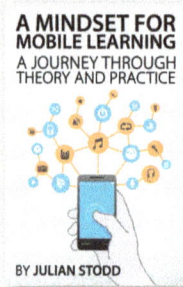

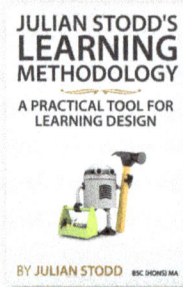

CERTIFICATIONS

In 2018 I launched the first Certification programme on *'Storytelling in Social Leadership'*. It's based upon *'Foundations'* and *'Techniques'*, which are practical and applied, and *'Experiments'*, which you learn to run in your own Organisation.

'Storytelling in Social Leadership'

'Leading with Trust'

'Community Building'

'Foundations of Social Leadership'

'Modern Learning Capabilities'

'Leading Through Change'

'Social Age Navigation'

Get in touch to find out more
www.seasaltlearning.com/certifications

SOCIAL LEADERSHIP DAILY

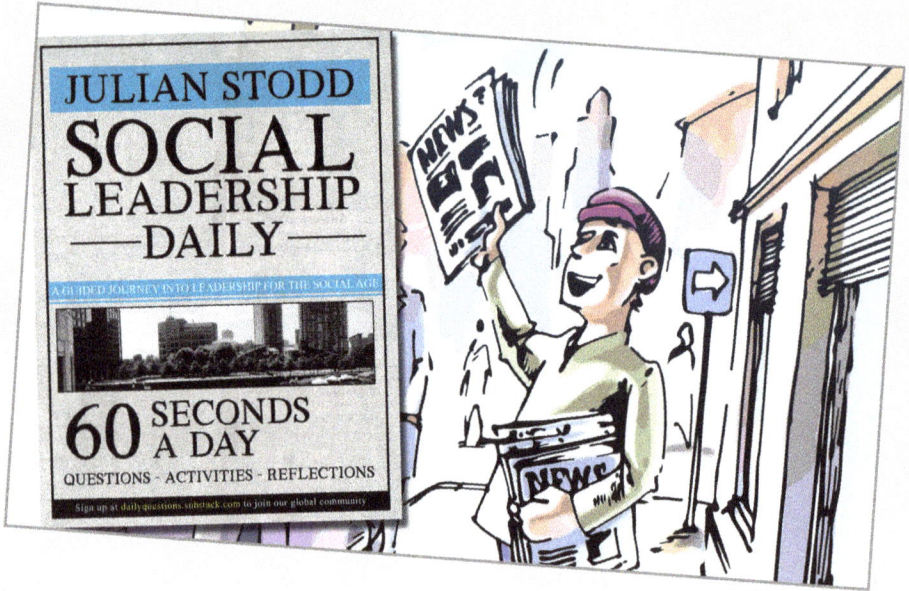

Daily questions, activities, and reflection in the arms of a global community of Explorers, putting Social Leadership into their everyday practice.

dailyquestions.substack.com

ABOUT SEA SALT LEARNING

We are a dynamic *Social Age startup:* living the values we speak. We are virtualised, global, inclusive, and agile. We are a core team of around twenty Crew Mates.

We are surrounded by a much larger layer of Social Age *'Explorers'*, people who are heavily involved in *'sense making'* around our core topics of Social Learning, Social Leadership, Change, Culture, and the Socially Dynamic Organisation.

Sea Salt Learning builds upon the work by Julian Stodd, author and explorer of the Social Age, recognised for his pioneering work in helping organisations to adapt to the new reality of the Social Age.

The *Sea Salt Research Hub* carries out original, creative, and large scale research, providing an evidence base for our work.

Sea Salt Publishing provides a curated body of books and online publications, exploring all aspects of the Social Age.

Sea Salt Digital provides our technical capability and build capacity for eLearning, mobile, video, and other forms of online learning.